Emerging Adulthood and Faith

Calvin Shorts

A series published by the Calvin College Press

Emerging Adulthood
and Faith

Jonathan P. Hill

Grand Rapids, Michigan • calvincollegepress.com

Published 2015 by the Calvin College Press
3201 Burton St. SE
Grand Rapids, MI 49546

Printed in the United States of America

Publisher's Cataloging-in-Publication data
Hill, Jonathan P.
  Emerging Adulthood and Faith / Jonathan P. Hill.
  pages   cm.
  ISBN 978-1-937555-11-5
  978-1-937555-12-2 (EPUB)
  Series : Calvin Shorts.
  Includes bibliographical references.
1. Youth --Religious life. 2. Youth --Conduct of life. 3. Church work with youth. 4. Church work with young adults. 5. Christian life.
I. Series. II. Title.
  BV4531.3 H55 2015
  248.8/34 --dc23   2015936324

Cover design: Robert Alderink

15 16 17 18 19 20   6 5 4 3 2 1

Contents

Series Editor's Foreword

Midway along the journey of our life
I woke to find myself in some dark woods,
For I had wandered off from the straight path.

So begins *The Divine Comedy,* a classic meditation on the Christian life, written by Dante Alighieri in the fourteenth century.

Dante's three images—a journey, a dark forest, and a perplexed pilgrim—still feel familiar today, don't they?

We can readily imagine our own lives as a series of journeys, not just the big journey from birth to death, but also all the little trips from home to school, from school to job, from place to place, from old friends to new. In fact, we often feel we are simultaneously on multiple journeys that tug us in diverse and sometimes opposing directions. We recognize those dark woods from fairy tales and nightmares and the all-too-real conundrums that crowd our everyday lives. No wonder we frequently feel perplexed. We wake up shaking our heads, unsure if we know how to live wisely today or tomorrow or next week.

This series has in mind just such perplexed pilgrims. Each book invites you, the reader, to walk alongside experienced guides who will help you understand the contours of the road as well as the surrounding landscape. They will cut back the underbrush, untangle myths and misconceptions, and suggest ways to move forward.

And they will do it in books intended to be read in an evening or during a flight. Calvin Shorts are designed not just for perplexed pilgrims, but also for busy ones. We live in a complex and changing world. We need nimble ways to acquire knowledge, skills, and wisdom. These books are one way to meet those needs.

John Calvin, after whom this series is named, recognized our pilgrim condition. "We are always on the road," he said, and although this road, this life, is full of perplexities, it is also "a gift of divine kindness which is not to be refused." Calvin Shorts takes as its starting point this claim that we are called to live well in a world that is both gift and challenge.

In *The Divine Comedy*, Dante's guide is Virgil, a wise but not omniscient mentor. So too, the authors in the Calvin Shorts series don't pretend to know it all. They, like you and me, are pilgrims. And they invite us to walk with them as together we seek to live more faithfully in this world that belongs to God.

Susan M. Felch
Executive Editor
The Calvin College Press

Additional Resources

Additional online resources for *Emerging Adulthood and Faith*, including large-scale graphs, are available at http://calvincollegepress.com/.

Additional information, references, and citations are included in the notes at the end of this book. Rather than using footnote numbers, these comments are keyed to phrases and page numbers.

Introduction

Are the Kids All Right?

The pews of Protestant churches today are filled with roughly the same percentage of emerging adults (age 18 to 29) as forty years ago. Surprised? You might be if you have spent any time in a Christian bookstore recently. Titles abound that warn of young people abandoning the faith at unprecedented rates. Millennials, they say, are a new breed of religious dropouts, with different priorities, attitudes, and aspirations than the generations that came before. And, when it comes to faith, they possess a deep skepticism of anything that smacks of inauthenticity and exclusion. The crisis is so acute, some have written, that today's young people will be the undoing of evangelicalism in America.

The goal of this book is to gain some perspective on emerging adults and their relationship to faith. To be clear, the problem is not a lack of data about young people. We have plenty of that. Rather, what is at issue is the way we make sense of these data. There is a decline, for example, in church involvement between the teenage years and the college years, but this fact alone does not tell a complete story.

Let me demonstrate. The following statements are both true:

- Protestant church attendance has remained nearly unchanged for forty years (and likely longer), while Catholic Mass attendance has seen steady decline over the same period.
- The percentage of emerging adults who identify as

Protestant has been in decline in recent years. The
percentage identifying as Catholic is unchanged.

These two facts are both true as well:

- Attending and graduating from college is associated
  with increased interest and participation in the faith
  of one's youth.
- Attending and graduating from college is associated
  with increased doubt about one's faith and results in a
  shift away from identification as evangelical Protestant.

At first glance, these paired statements may seem
contradictory, but they are not. By paying attention to the
larger social and historical context, these individual facts
become part of a coherent story. Unfortunately, this big
picture account is rarely examined in the books targeting
concerned parents, pastors, and priests. Many latch onto
a single statistic (e.g., the rise of young people with no
religion, or the sharp decline in church attendance between
adolescence and emerging adulthood) and weave their own
story of exodus and decline.

I do *not* think these authors are intentionally overstating
what is going on, but two current tendencies in writing
about emerging adult faith are almost certainly part of the
problem. The first is the overemphasis on generational
analysis. It is hard to find a book on young people today
that does not focus on the distinctiveness of Millennials.
The second is the tendency to analyze emerging adult faith
through the lens of individual stories. Neither focus is bad
in and of itself, but both have the tendency to distort the
overall picture if they are not balanced by historical, social,
and developmental context.

TALKING 'BOUT GENERATIONS

It's probably not an overstatement to say that nearly every book about the religious faith of young people today has focused on their distinctiveness as a social generation. The most frequent label is "Millennials," but they have also been called Generation Y, Generation Next, and the Echo Boomers. The exact year that marks the beginning of this group of young people varies from study to study, but we can think of Millennials as those born after 1980. The question remains, however, whether or not isolating young people as a group, treating them as a distinct generation, and comparing them to older Americans, is the best way to make sense of the changing religious landscape in the United States. It's certainly a useful method some of the time, though not the only one at our disposal. And, if we only use this tool while neglecting others, we are bound to make some serious errors.

Differences are fascinating. There is no compelling "story" about generations when the old and young are similar. And yet, on a number of attitudes and beliefs, young and old *are* remarkably similar. For example, a quick peek at the last few General Social Surveys (GSS) administered between 2006 and 2012, reveals that there are virtually no age differences when assessing beliefs about capital punishment—a hot button political issue that commonly separates conservatives and liberals. Opinions about whether abortion should be legal also do not show clear age differences. Faith in the American Dream—affirming that hard work, as opposed to luck or help, is how people primarily get ahead in life—is also virtually identical across age groups (and is unchanged over the nearly forty years the question has been asked). While these generational

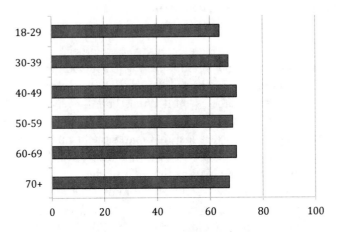

Figure 1. Percent favoring capital punishment by age
Source: GSS, 2006–2012

commonalities are not going to make headlines, we should be aware of the similarities and take them into account.

Still, there are a number of attitudes, beliefs, and practices where real and substantial differences between age groups emerge. This would seem to clearly demonstrate that there are generational differences, right? Not so fast. The difficulty here is that taking a snapshot at one single point in time does not adequately capture the full picture. Let me demonstrate with a simple example. If we examine the 2012 GSS, we find that the percentage of American young people under age 30 who report praying daily is 39 percent. Moving up the age ladder to those in their forties, 66 percent report praying daily. Finally, for those in later life, age 70 and above, we see that 71 percent claim to pray every day. This, it would initially appear, is the result of generational differences. But it's not. If you back up to the first year this question was asked in the GSS, in 1983,

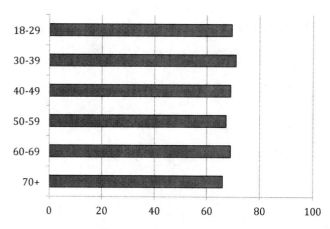

Figure 2. Percent believing in the American Dream by age
Source: GSS, 2006–2012

you find the following: 42 percent of 18–29 year olds pray daily; 60 percent of those between the ages of 40–49 pray every day, and 68 percent of those aged 70 and above report engaging in daily prayer. These are very similar numbers to the 2012 survey results.

At any given moment, age differences between people can be the result of some combination of what demographers refer to as age, period, and cohort effects. These terms are used to describe changes associated with biographical time (age), changes associated with historical shifts (period), and changes associated with generational differences (cohort). While there are some very real statistical challenges to estimating the unique contribution of each of these factors, disaggregating these trends is essential to understanding what is occurring.

There are some changes that *do* appear to be primarily driven by generational differences, but a large number

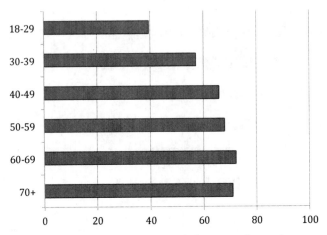

Figure 3. Percent who report praying daily or more by age in 2012
Source: GSS, 2012

of changes seem instead to be associated with aging or
cultural transitions that cut across generations. Sorting
through these variations helps us to better understand our
present moment and to develop more reasonable expectations about the direction of the future.

THE POWER OF STORIES

The second tendency we need to be careful about is our
attraction to stories. Stories are the way we make sense of
reality. We tell stories to orient ourselves to the present, to
make sense of the past, and to anticipate the future. Stories
are indispensable to being human. They allow us to know
the world in ways that isolated "facts" cannot. A short fable
can give us glimpses of truth that a lengthy analytical tome
can't capture. At the same time, stories can act as powerful blinders. Precisely because they hold such power, they

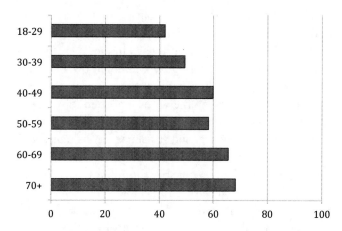

Figure 4. Percent who report praying daily or more by age in 1983
Source: GSS, 1983

cut us off from alternative ways of seeing the world. They generate tunnel vision.

Stories need to be balanced by good, careful social science. Sociologists are sometimes accused of being cold-hearted number crunchers, and this critique is true some of the time. When sociologists spend hours in the company of variables and correlations instead of living and breathing persons, they can sometimes generate absurd explanations of the social world. Our personal knowledge of the world—the kind that is captured best in stories—is indispensable for getting at the truth.

But this is also true: our individual experience of the world is limited in important ways. Our particular "social location," the confluence of multiple identities that we all juggle (such as gender, race, social class, religion, politics), results in our experience of the world being filtered in particular ways. Our own personal encounter with the world is not the same as our neighbor's, and is certainly not identical to the experience of a person who lives half way around the world, or a century ago in time. Good social science allows us to take a step back from our own experiences, providing data that can give us glimpses of powerful social forces we would otherwise be blinded to. These forces are the background to our lives, though we are often unaware of their influence. Social science can help us see these contexts.

To be clear, the data do not speak for themselves. Social scientists, like everyone else, still need to make sense of the world in narrative form in order to construct a plausible account of reality. This is what I try to do in this book. And, yes, social scientists—like everyone else—must (and should) use their own personal experiences to construct this account. But good social science balances these stories with stubborn data that sometimes do not conform to our preconceived notion of the world. It is not uncommon to be surprised at what the data tell us and be forced to reconstruct the account so that it best fits this new information.

If there is a single complaint I have about many of the findings that are "out there," it is that they lack this fuller context. The camera is always zoomed in a little too close as we hear story after individual story. Even when we are presented with survey data about attitudes and beliefs, they are not typically used to interrogate the broader context. Instead, these data are most frequently used to create typologies of this or that category of emerging adult but are rarely analyzed to account for the social and cultural forces at work in producing these categories to begin with. This use of survey data is ultimately limited.

My goal in this short book is to zoom out a bit from the individual stories. I hope by doing so that we can see that some concerns articulated by commentators are probably misplaced. At the same time, I hope we can see that other concerns, ones we may not have considered fully in the past, deserve our attention.

WHAT'S NEXT?

In this book, we will look at three big issues. The first is a reexamination of the religious practice and identity of young people. Much of the current crop of books on emerging adult faith begins with the premise that Millennials are abandoning Christian practice and identification. But is this true? What can we tell by taking a longer look at the trends, and what are the factors that are driving the trends? I will argue that the standard exodus narrative turns out to be quite flawed.

The second chapter takes up the issue of higher education. College has long been thought of as corrosive to faith. The influence of secular faculty, the absence of adult supervision, the religious pluralism of the campus, and the critical stance of liberal education itself have all been targeted as potential sources of conflict with faith. Again, is this true? We need to examine trends over time, as well as changes that occur for those who never attend college at all. College ultimately has a complex relationship with student faith, but the story of unilateral religious decline is clearly false.

The third chapter turns to science. Two dominant narratives exist about the faith of young people and science. On the one hand, some propose that the reason many young people experience a crisis of faith is because they have compromised their beliefs by succumbing to the secularist assumptions of modern science. Others hold that the

rejection of mainstream science by many conservative Protestants has set their children up for a future crisis of faith
in college. Both of these positions assume that science is a
primary front in the battle for the souls of adolescents and
emerging adults. But is this true? The potential for conflict
between faith and science turns out to be a minor concern
for most believers. Further, changing beliefs about science
are not associated with major changes in religious faith.

Finally, the book closes by exploring why the various
decline narratives hold such power and suggests ways the
Church might care for its adolescents and emerging adults.
Here I introduce the concept of social scripts that many
young people follow. Most young people engage in a fairly
narrow range of options when it comes to their faith, and
articulate a fairly narrow range of reasons for these behaviors. How should the Church respond to the dominant
faith scripts that young people hold to? The goal is not to
develop a full-fledged program for youth faith development,
but to explore a set of ideas that might help point toward
some successful strategies.

1

Should They Stay or Should They Go?

Make no mistake about it, young people are leaving churches. The exodus begins in their teenage years and continues into their early twenties. And the decline is not insubstantial either. If the ideal behavior for most faith traditions is weekly church attendance, then somewhere between 50 and 70 percent of teenagers who were regularly in church on Sunday morning are no longer attending by their early twenties. One of the best surveys of youth religion finds that 42 percent of teenagers (age 13 to 17) attend church weekly. By the time the same teenagers are college-aged (18 to 23), the figure is only 20 percent. Figure 5 shows information from yet another large national survey which demonstrates that when weekly church attendance is first measured at age 15, the decline is already in full swing with a little less than 40 percent categorized as regular attenders. Every year this decline continues until it reaches a low of slightly more than 15 percent, and by age 20 it begins to level off.

What about the religious traditions with which young people identify? In the United States, this is most commonly a Protestant or Catholic identity, although various minority religious groups are on the rise. Young people today, however, are more likely to have no religious affiliation than in the past. According to the 2012 General Social Survey, about one-third of Americans under the age of 30 claim no religious affiliation. The comparable figure is 13 percent for those aged 50 and above.

To understand these trends a little better, let's take a

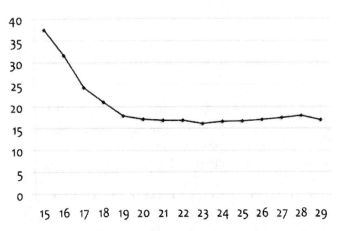

Figure 5. Percent attending religious services weekly or more from age 15 to 29
Source: National Longitudinal Survey of Youth 1997, 2000–2010

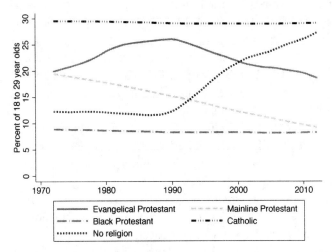

Figure 6. Religious tradition of 18–29 year olds, 1972–2012
Source: GSS, 1972–2012

closer look at the under 30s over time. The GSS has been asking about religious identity since 1972. According to Figure 6, both Black Protestants and Catholics have remained remarkably stable as a percentage of all 18 to 29 year olds for the past forty years (although the stability of Catholics is actually a more complicated story, given the influx of immigration from predominately Catholic countries). The significant change is clearly happening among Protestants and the nonaffiliated. Mainline Protestants—those who identify with large, theologically liberal, Protestant denominations such as the United Methodist Church, Episcopal Church, and Evangelical Lutheran Church in America—have been in decline since the survey began. Evangelical Protestants—represented by more theologically conservative groups such as Southern Baptists, Pentecostals, and many non-denominational congregations—grew in size until around 1990, but then began a decline from more than one-quarter of this population to less than 20 percent. Also around 1990, the percent claiming no religion climbs from approximately 12 percent to nearly 30 percent.

ARE MILLENNIAL EMERGING ADULTS DIFFERENT?

All of the numbers cited above have been used to suggest that the future of both mainline and evangelical Protestants in the US is bleak. But these numbers need context. Let's start by looking at an alternative statistic—one that, as far as I know, has not been widely distributed. It's the statistic I quoted at the beginning of this book: roughly the same percentage of young people are sitting in the pews (or folding chairs) of Protestant churches today as were there in the 1970s. About 12-13 percent of 18 to 29 year olds attend a Protestant church every week. If this is so, why the drop in

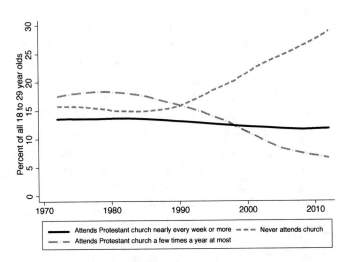

Figure 7. Protestant church attendance of 18-29 year olds, 1972-2012
Source: GSS, 1972-2012

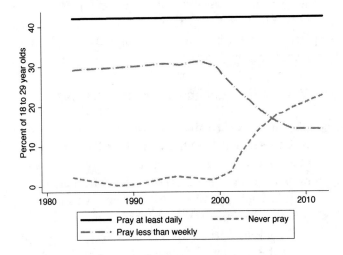

Figure 8. Frequency of prayer of 18-29 year olds, 1983-2012
Source GSS, 1983-2012

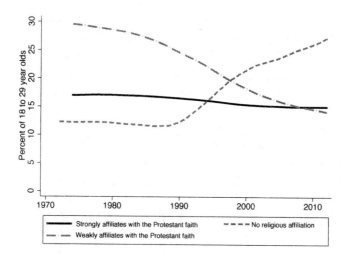

Figure 9. *Strength of religious affiliation of 18–29 year olds, 1972–2012*
Source: GSS, 1972–2012

evangelical and mainline Protestant identity and the significant increase in the number of non-affiliates? We can start to figure this out if we take a closer look at the margins. Figure 7 shows this. While the regular Protestant attenders are stable, those who only attend once or twice a year begin to decline by the late 1980s; at the same time, those who never attend double in size from 15 to 30 percent.

These very same patterns can be seen with other measures of religious practice and identity. The percent that report praying every day is constant over time (Figure 8). A little more than 40 percent of those under 30 say they do this regularly. Those who pray only occasionally (less than once a week) begin to drastically decline in number around the year 2000; while those who never pray skyrockets around the same time. The strength of religious affiliation looks remarkably similar (Figure 9). The percentages who strongly affiliate with an evangelical or mainline Protestant faith is constant over time in this age group (roughly 15 to 17 percent). Those who weakly identify with a Protestant faith are only half of what they used to be, while those who have no religious identity, as we have seen, have more than doubled.

At least among Protestants, every concerned parent and pastor should know this: The percentage of young people with a strong Protestant identity, and the percentage who regularly practice their faith publicly and privately has barely budged over the past forty years. They are in your churches, youth groups, and Bible studies. Yes, something has been happening at the margins, but the center has held.

THE SOCIAL SOURCES OF THESE CHANGES

How are we to make sense of all of this? Let's explore a few of the broader social trends that are likely culprits. First, there is an important story to be told about the cultural disestablishment of Protestantism in the United States: The faithful are still there, but the nominal are shrinking fast, and the ranks of the unaffiliated are growing. This trend is particularly noticeable among young people today. Rare is the young person today who feels the need to identify as Lutheran and attend services on Christmas and Easter for purely social or cultural reasons. In the past there was a benefit to this identity—a pressure to be seen as the "right" type of religious person in the eyes of others, but this social norm is fading fast.

Yet, this institutional decline and waning Protestant cultural power does not necessarily mean that liberal Protestantism has somehow lost its hold over how Americans think about religion. It may, in fact, be precisely the opposite. Some have argued that the institutional decline has come with a cultural victory. At an organizational-level, the old mainline denominations have seen drastic declines in membership since their height in the 1950s. But, at a cultural level, the values that are central to liberal Protestantism—tolerance, individualism, pluralism, democracy, and critical inquiry—have been absorbed into the mainstream. In an ironic twist, these values actually work to undermine the organizational vitality of liberal Protestantism (after all, why have an organization to support values that have become dominant in public life?). As the logic of these values is applied to ever-wider circles of society, the cultural playing field becomes leveled. The social benefit of belonging to certain religious organizations weakens, and the importance of tolerating (maybe even celebrating) believers of all faiths, *including those without a faith*, grows.

Second, in addition to the diffusion of liberal Protestant cultural values, there is the gradual impact resulting from increases in interfaith social relationships. Interfaith marriage has become increasingly common. Nearly half of marriages in the first decade of the twenty-first century were between different faiths (including Protestants and Catholics, or unions between mainline Protestants and evangelical Protestants) while before the 1960s, this was only about 20 percent. The same data do not exist on interfaith friendships over time, but they are almost certainly more common today than they once were, with the majority of Americans reporting having a friend who belongs to another faith. As the religious barriers to social relationships decline, the experience of knowing someone of an alternative faith increases. Political scientists Robert Putnam and David Campbell refer to this as the "Aunt Susan Principle" and the "My Friend Al Principle." This change in the typical

American's social network increases tolerance for other faiths. After all, Aunt Susan and Al are both good people and cannot possibly be destined for hell in the minds of most. When family and friends cut across religious boundaries, the exclusive claims of religion become harder to believe. So, while slow shifts in cultural values have opened up the possibility of interfaith marriages and friendships, the social networks resulting from these changes further entrench the value of tolerance for all faith groups.

Third, there is a weakening of trust in public institutions. Young people are routinely suspicious of public pronouncements from government, big business, media, and the Church in a way that their grandparents would not have been. In short, this is not simply about religion, but about public trust and goodwill extended to institutions more generally. As a side note, the most noticeable decline in institutional trust is occurring among those who do not have a college education, but we will take this up further in the next chapter. Increasingly, people live their lives outside the authority of public institutions, including the Church.

All three of these factors result in the establishment of a growing non-religious sector of the public, particularly in the younger segment of the population. While this sector is new historically, it comes almost entirely at the expense of cultural Protestantism: Those who were once weakly committed no longer feel the need to maintain their religious affiliation.

WHAT HAPPENS TO RELIGION DURING EMERGING ADULTHOOD?

None of these data negate the fact that emerging adulthood is still a particularly low religious point during the life course. Although this has been true for some time, it is little consolation for the concerned parent, pastor, or priest who sees and hears of emerging adults dropping out of church. But how should we understand this exodus?

First, let's take a closer look at the percentage who actually drop out. If we are examining self-reported disaffiliation, the vast majority of emerging adults quite clearly do *not* disaffiliate. Four out of five emerging adults raised within a religious affiliation maintain a religious affiliation. Even if we look at church attendance, the proportion of regularly attending adolescents who functionally "quit" church as emerging adults (stop going entirely or only attend a few times per year at most) is around one-third. Should this be a concern? Of course, but this is hardly the 70 or 80 percent figure that we sometimes hear.

Second, it matters a great deal whether these changes represent a permanent departure from personal faith and participation in the Church—or only a temporary hiatus. It is well documented that many young people return to regular worship during adulthood, particularly when they marry and begin forming their own families. If we imagine the scenario of these individuals returning to early adolescent rates of worship attendance after marriage and children, then we would expect to see fairly stable rates of overall worship attendance in the population (with slight variations depending on the size of birth cohorts). If, on the other hand, the departure is permanent, and average rates do not recover to early adolescent levels, then there should be a slow decline as older birth cohorts are replaced by younger ones. We could ask the question this way: Is decline in church attendance primarily about general aging patterns of religious participation? Or is it primarily about differences between generations?

For Protestants, the proportion of the population which reports attending church regularly has remained remarkably stable over many decades. Using Gallup polls (since the late 1950s) and the General Social Survey (beginning in 1972), we find that about 40 to 50 percent of evangelical Protestants consistently report attending church nearly every week or more, while around 30 percent of mainline Protestants report the same. Again, those who "never" attend church have certainly been on the rise, but the weekly attenders are quite stable. These self-reports are almost certainly overestimates, but they are probably consistent overestimates. Catholics, on the other hand, have seen a steady decline over this same period. The best estimates from the Gallup data tell us more than 75 percent of Catholics attended Mass at least weekly in the late 1950s. In 1972, when the General Social Survey first began, 61 percent attended Mass roughly weekly or more. In 2010, only 29 percent of Catholics attended at this rate.

So what does this mean? Without going into the details of how sociologists conduct cohort analysis, we can safely say that Catholic Mass attendance varies substantially by birth cohort, while Protestant church attendance varies mostly by age. In other words, Catholics are seeing generational decline while Protestants are not. As they age, Protestants *are* returning as best as we can tell. Longitudinal data that follow the same respondents over time (one data set that starts with a baseline of high school seniors in 1965 and one with adolescents in 1979) confirm that Catholic trajectories are distinctly different from Protestant ones. Catholics are not returning to their childhood levels of Mass attendance. These data suggest that the exodus from the Church is largely a Catholic phenomenon.

CONCLUSION

Let's step back a moment and take stock of what we can say. First, although the number of young people with no religious affiliation has increased (substantially) during the past two decades, this is mostly about the changing cultural and political meanings of belonging to a Protestant tradition. The wrong conclusion to draw is that the rise of the religious "nones" is coming at the expense of the churched. This is simply not true. Second, at least in terms of religious participation, there is no evidence that the current crop of young people (Millennials) are somehow drastically different from previous generations. There are undoubtedly subtle shifts in how young people think and talk about their religious faith, but this is not translating into noticeably different rates of religious participation. The most noticeable historical change in religious participation is the decline in the total number of individuals who attend church only a few times per year. Third, the majority of young people who have been raised in the Church decline in their participation during late adolescence and early emerging adulthood, but the majority of these individuals are not permanently "leaving" the Church in any meaningful sense of the term. Rather, they are participating less frequently, and, for both evangelical and mainline Protestants, they historically return to pre-decline levels of participation later in life.

Let me end this chapter with two important caveats. While it is important not to overemphasize Millennials as something new and different, it is also important to recognize that this is a relatively brief snippet of history we are examining. Even the concept of adolescence is a relatively recent cultural invention, let alone "emerging adulthood." The decline of faith, practice, and belief during this period of the life course *is* likely something relatively new in the long history of Christendom, even though we obviously do not have the social survey data to back this up. At the same time, we should be careful not to overestimate some sort of "golden era" of faith from which we've fallen. Public practice and belief have likely always fallen well short of the standards set by religious authorities.

Second, even though the exodus from church is much more apparent in the Catholic tradition, this does not mean all is well for Protestants. The leaving of many young people from the Church, even if temporary, is a very real loss. It is also important to note that the future of young Protestants is still unknown. The ability to document certain patterns in the past is no guarantee of their continuance into the future. If we look at our present historical moment, there are a number of cultural and economic forces working against returning to regular participation in public worship. The median age at first marriage has continued to rise since its low at the middle of the last century. In 2011, the median age at first marriage for men was 28.7 and 26.5 for women (still considerably lower than many Western European countries). This, accompanied with at least half of young people cohabiting before marriage, and an increase in the number choosing to never marry, means the pull of family formation back into church may be weaker than in the past. In addition, economic changes over the last few decades have increased the need for higher education and delayed the establishment of long-term, stable careers. This means that the transition to stable adulthood, and the return to regular participation in a place of worship, may be less of a given than in the recent past. Still, we should be cautious in jumping to the conclusion that young people, particularly Protestants, who leave the pews today will never return.

2

Losing Their Religion . . .
in College

We have already seen that disengagement from the Church is a complex phenomenon. But everyone knows that higher education is the enemy of faith, right? Young believers innocently head off to college or university only to encounter serious challenges to their beliefs. Perhaps they are sucked into the party scene with its abundance of alcohol and sex. Perhaps they encounter such a diversity of faith traditions and worldviews that their former beliefs seem parochial and naïve. Perhaps they take a course on the Bible that undermines a high view of scripture, or a biology class that explains how divine guidance is unnecessary to produce the varieties of life on earth. College certainly seems like a dangerous place for young Christians.

Social scientists have been studying the influence of college on faith and practice over the last several years with some surprising results. While the stories of individual faith loss are real and deserve our attention, there is little evidence of widespread disaffection from the faith as a result of secular higher education.

Some of the first social scientific studies of college and faith compared first year college students with graduating seniors. The general finding was that seniors were less orthodox on measures of Christian belief and practiced their faith (both publicly and privately) less frequently than first year students. One reasonable conclusion would be that college is exerting a secularizing effect on students. The longer they attend, the more their faith is chiseled away.

But this is hard to square with another way of assessing social scientific data. More recent studies have used national surveys of the entire adult population, such as the General Social Survey used in the previous chapter, to examine the correlation between measures of religious faith and measures of educational attainment. These results *don't* show a clear-cut pattern of secularism associated with attending and graduating from college. College graduates are actually *more* likely to practice their faith and say it is important in their daily life. They are no more likely to disaffiliate from a religious faith, although they do appear more likely to shy away from exclusivist claims about the Bible and more prone to switch to a mainline Protestant denomination. Why the different results?

There are several factors at work here. The first method—comparing freshman to seniors—makes the assumption that the college experience accounts for the change. But we know this cannot be entirely true since we also see declines in religious practice and belief during this same age range (roughly age 18 to 22) among young people not in college. Using this first method of assessing only college students, there is no way to separate out the college influence from changes rooted in other cultural and developmental changes. Studies need to compare college students to those who are *not* in college to identify the relative differences in change. It might seem strange, but college could theoretically have a positive impact on faith even when there is an apparent decline on most religious measures between freshman and senior year.

The second method—using general population surveys—ignores the fact that those who attend and graduate from college may be different from the rest of the population for reasons that have little to do with college itself. For instance, they could have very different religious identities and practices to begin with. This is commonly referred to as selection bias. While there are some ways to mitigate the influence of selection bias, there is no foolproof method for ruling this out in general population surveys.

The third factor to consider is the sheer complexity of the relationship between higher education and faith. Higher education has gone through substantial historical shifts that may mean the religious impact of a generation ago no longer holds today—a possibility that we will explore in a moment. On top of this, the widely varying types of institutions and educational models are unlikely to be uniform in their influence on faith. Add this to the diversity of personal backgrounds existing in the student body, and we have the recipe to undermine any single story about higher education and religious faith. This is not to say that no general patterns exist. It is simply a recognition that any account of college and faith needs to specify the conditions under which the relationship holds.

Is There an Overall Secularizing Effect from College?

Let's do our best to unpack some of these issues. Can we detect any overall influence from college in the entire emerging adult population? To do this well, we will look at a different type of survey that doesn't fall prey to some of the problems with the research already cited.

To really isolate the impact of college, we need nationally representative panel data. Panel surveys, unlike standard cross-sectional surveys, follow the same group of people over time. If we begin following a national sample of adolescents, we can measure their faith at multiple points in time. Some of these young people will go to college while others will enter the workforce, and some may do neither. This type of data is precisely what has been analyzed in recent years.

The results are somewhat surprising. For the most part, going to college does *not* substantially alter the religious trajectories of young people. An analysis of the best survey for measuring this impact, the National Study of Youth and Religion, finds there are no substantial difference between college students and other young people across more than a dozen measures of religious identity, practice, and beliefs (once their faith as teenagers is taken into account). Out of twenty-three measures I examined, fifteen show no statistical significant differences. These measures include belief in God, closeness to God, belief in an afterlife, belief in a future judgment day, importance of faith in daily life, frequency of prayer and Bible reading, identifying as "spiritual but not religious," and several indicators of religious exclusivism (e.g., can someone practice more than one faith? Is there only one true religion?). College does not seem to alter these religious trajectories. And, among the few differences that we can find—and I will show them in more detail in just a moment—the results do not unilaterally support a secularization narrative.

ACCOUNTING FOR NOTHING

Before discussing these few differences, it is worth considering the non-findings in more detail. What can account for the general lack of religious influence from college for recent graduates? Shouldn't the pluralism of belief systems on many campuses, the secular commitments of many university faculty, the hermeneutics of suspicion that animates much of science and philosophy, and the student party culture (to name just a few potential secularizing sources) undermine a commitment to religious faith? I am not trying to claim that these factors are never stumbling blocks for the religiously committed on campus; I am quite certain that they are for some. But we need to recognize that most students do not come to campus with strong religious commitments in the first place. Sociologist Tim Clydesdale has studied students the first year out of high school and finds that most new college students tend to take their religious identity and place it in a metaphorical "lockbox." Young people primarily follow a script that tells them religion has very little to do with this phase of their life and can be safely and temporarily set aside. Similarly, Donna Freitas, in her study of sexual activity and religion on college campuses finds that most students (with the exception of students attending evangelical colleges) see no real connection between their sex life and their faith. If religious identity is fragmented and private for most 18 to 23 year olds, then why should we expect college to have any influence?

THE EXCEPTIONS TO THE RULE

With the "no effect" story as the default backdrop, let's take a closer look at the exceptions, which can be classified into two groups. On the one hand, college appears to have a positive influence on institutional belonging. The most notable example of this is church attendance. Figure 10 compares those who have never gone to college (both high school graduates and high school dropouts, but not anyone currently enrolled in high school who wouldn't have had the chance to go to college), current college students attending non-religious institutions, and college graduates.

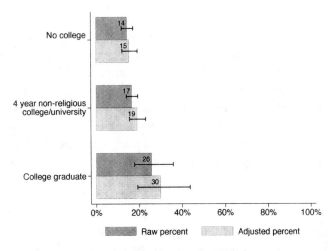

Figure 10. Percent of 18–23 year olds attending worship services weekly by educational attainment
Source: National Study of Youth and Religion 2002–3, 2007–8

Some emerging adults do not fit into these categories, but comparing these particular groups allows us to assess whether education leaves a religious mark of any kind. The top bar for each group shows the "raw" percentage—the percentage within each group who attend church weekly when measured at age 18 to 23. The bottom bar ("adjusted percent") controls for the frequency of church attendance when they were age 13 to 17, as well as for other religious and demographic factors. In this case, these additional control factors make little difference to the general findings. Put simply, the graph tells us that the further one has gone educationally by age 18 to 23, the more likely she is to be attending a place of worship regularly.

Similar trends can be found if we examine those who do not identify with any faith (most likely among those who have *not* attended or graduated from college) and those who believe a religious congregation is necessary to be truly religious (most likely among those who *have* attended or graduated from college). These all suggest that attending and graduating from college results in young people identifying more with the institutional side of religious life.

Again, it is worth pausing to consider why this might be. Given the lack of increase (or decrease) in most other measures of religious belief and practice, it seems unlikely that the increased institutional commitment is due to an intensified personal faith. The more likely explanation, I would contend, relies upon social class distinctions in trust and on participation in mainstream social institutions. Individuals with a college education are more likely to participate in all sorts of social institutions and aspects of public life—religious and nonreligious. The disenchantment (and often distrust) of mainstream social institutions has grown disproportionately among the working classes and those without a college education. Marriage and family life, political participation and volunteering, religious participation—all of this has remained relatively stable over time for college graduates but has been declining among those without college degrees. College, increasingly, is the link to middle-class life. Religious involvement is just one part of the middle class package.

The other notable exception is the slight decline in some measures of supernatural beliefs associated with attending and graduating from college. In the NSYR data, the decline is associated with measures of miracles, angels, and demons (but *not* belief in a personal God, a future judgment day, or an afterlife). Figure 11 shows the percentage of respondents who "definitely" believe in miracles, by college status. Even when controlling for what the respondent believed at age 13

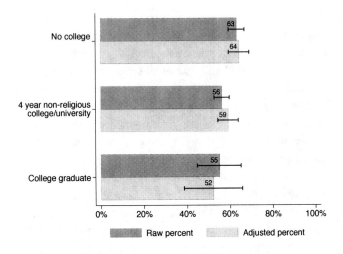

Figure 11. Percent of 18–23 year olds who definitely believe in miracles by educational attainment
Source: National Study of Youth and Religion 2002–3, 2007–8

to 17 (this is what the "adjusted percentages" account for), the gap between never going to college and graduating from college is about 12 percentage points (64 percent versus 52 percent). Likewise, if we ask those who identify as religious if they have had any doubts about their religion, those who attend and graduate from college report at least having a few doubts at a higher rate (Figure 12).

So what can we conclude? College is most certainly not a catalyst for total disaffiliation or atheism. By most accounts, higher education actually strengthens affiliation and identification with the institutional side of religious life. Nevertheless, there are some types of beliefs, particularly the belief that supernatural forces and entities are active in the world, that appear to decline because of attending college.

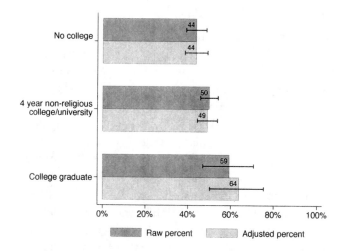

Figure 12. Percent of 18–23 year olds who have had at least a few doubts about their faith by educational attainment (only includes those who identify with a faith tradition)
Source: National Study of Youth and Religion 2002-3, 2007-8

Still, by any stretch of the imagination, college is not a unilateral secularizing force. In fact, the substantial declines in religious practices documented in the previous chapter have very little to do with college.

RELIGIOUS STUDENTS IN COLLEGE

But this does not settle the matter entirely. Perhaps college is not poison to faith for most people, but that is because most do not enter it with anything like a robust, vibrant faith life. What about the impact of college on the highly religious? To investigate this, I've restricted the sample to those who attended church weekly and who reported their faith was "very" or "extremely" important as adolescents—a little less than one-third of the full sample. Using the same methods and the same twenty-three measures of religious belief, practice, and identity, the results are nearly identical to the full sample. Seventeen of the twenty-three measures show no significant changes in religion based on whether or not emerging adults attended or graduated from college. The few that do show significant changes follow the familiar pattern outlined in the previous section: supernatural beliefs decline as a result of attending and graduating from college while institutional commitment is stronger for those who attended and graduated from college. The only notable difference in the religious sample centers around relatively low levels of "spiritual but not religious" identification among those who attend and graduate from college. Religious adolescents who do *not* attend college are more than twice as likely to identify as "spiritual but not religious" at age 18 to 23, even after their identification as adolescents is controlled for.

Why doesn't college have a negative effect for these highly religious students? While it is impossible to know solely from the survey data, these findings are less surprising than they may appear at first glance. We can reasonably suppose that religious students coming to a secular campus will be very aware of their minority status. Those determined to hold on to their faith will make it a priority to identify likeminded others (perhaps through parachurch organizations such as Cru or Intervarsity) and develop a general posture of guardedness and readiness for potential conflict. Christian Smith has made this argument about evangelicals in American culture more generally. From a social psychological perspective, embracing a minority identity allows for a clear "us" and a clear "them." Intergroup conflict only serves to strengthen intragroup solidarity.

The diversity of the student population on most secular campuses, then, allows students of all types to find their place and reinforce their identity against the other groups on campus.

RELIGIOUSLY AFFILIATED COLLEGES AND UNIVERSITIES

To this point, I have purposefully avoided analyzing religiously affiliated colleges and universities because most concerns about the negative influence of higher education are not targeted at these institutions. After all, many religiously affiliated institutions have religious and spiritual formation as an explicit goal. But do they succeed on this front? I think the answer is likely "yes," but we need better research to confirm this conclusion. In the NSYR data, those who attend religious colleges and universities *do* show considerable positive effects for religious practice (church attendance, Bible reading, frequency of prayer), and the negative effects on supernatural beliefs are not evident at these institutions. Unfortunately, there is not an adequate way to separate out the *type* of religious institution (e.g. Catholic, mainline Protestant, evangelical Protestant, Mormon, Jewish, etc.) without reducing the sample size of survey respondents to an unacceptably low level. This is one of the difficulties of relying on a national sample, since small subpopulations that are of interest to the researchers are sometimes out of reach.

One alternative is to use data that oversamples on religiously affiliated colleges. The Spirituality in Higher Education survey data, collected by the Higher Education Research Institute at UCLA, relies upon a college-based sample. Although these data run into some of the difficulties mentioned at the outset of this chapter (namely there is no non-college sample to compare to), they do have adequate numbers of students attending Catholic, evangelical Protestant, and non-evangelical Protestant colleges to compare to respondents attending other institutions. Students were measured as incoming freshman and again during the second semester of their junior year. On every measure of religious practice and identity, individuals attending evangelical Protestant colleges decline considerably less than their counterparts at other schools. For example, only 2 percent of students at evangelical colleges who enter with a religious affiliation report having no affiliation by the end of their junior year (compared to 8 percent at public institutions). Eighty percent of individuals at evangelical colleges who were attending religious services "frequently" as incoming students are still attending frequently by the end of their junior year. Only 47 percent of undergraduates at public institutions are doing the same. Seventy-three percent of students at evangelical colleges who prayed daily continued to do so, while 56 percent of those at public institutions still reported daily prayer. In all of these instances, students attending Catholic and non-evangelical church-related colleges and universities are much closer to the public university students than the individuals at evangelical colleges.

Does this mean that the evangelical colleges are the sole cause of these higher rates of religious practice and identification? Probably not. These students could be different in a number of ways that the survey does not easily capture (e.g., more supportive religious households, higher religious expectations from parents and home churches, youth pastors who stay in contact with them, friends from home who support them spiritually, etc.). On the other hand, it would be extremely unlikely that the curricular and co-curricular aspects of evangelical colleges have *no* influence on these types of outcomes. By most accounts, it is a safe bet that evangelical colleges are relatively successful in nurturing faith among their students. The success rate at Catholic and other church-related institutions is mixed at best.

HISTORICAL CONTEXT

But what about placing this (non)finding in historical context? While college does not unilaterally undermine faith in any straightforward fashion for current students and graduates, perhaps it did in the recent past. Higher education has rapidly expanded since the 1960s when some of the earliest studies of faith and college first emerged. Not only this, but incoming students have different expectations of their college experience today compared to several decades ago. Two sociological studies from the 1980s tracked the religious beliefs and practices of students over time at specific institutions. Students at Marquette (a Catholic institution) and students at Dartmouth (an elite secular university with Protestant roots) both exhibited declines in the percent who believed and practiced traditional faiths from the early 1960s to the 1970s. However, both campuses also saw an increase in faith and practice by the time surveys were administered in the 1980s. Still, these studies tell us little about the changing impact of college on faith over time because of the narrow sample and absence of a non-college comparison group (it is quite possible that all emerging adults were becoming more religiously traditional in the 1980s and higher education had nothing to do with this).

One way we can assess these data is by looking at a survey that repeats questions on religion and educational attainment over time—like the General Social Survey (administered since 1972). We can pool all of the years of the GSS together and separate out respondents by the decade within which they were born (ranging from before 1920 to 1980 and after). We can then measure the difference between those who have a four-year college degree and those who don't by birth cohort. If the gap is positive—if college graduates measure higher—then the bar graphs are positive; if the gap is negative—with college graduates measuring lower—then the bar graphs are negative. This allows us to see whether the impact of college trends are changing over time. Still, as before, we cannot be sure whether the gap is due to college or due to initial differences in the types of people who went on to receive a college education. To help mitigate the second possibility, I include adjusted differences that control for household background factors, including measures of religious tradition and religious fundamentalism at age 16. I also control for gender, age, race/ethnicity, and parents' educational attainment. The final results tell us that college, for those born in early decades, was more of a secularizing force in the past than it is today. The church attendance "boost" from college was much smaller historically than it is currently. Moreover, earlier generations were more likely to disaffiliate if they went to college, while those born in the 1970s are actually more likely to disaffiliate if they *don't* go to college. Likewise, in earlier generations, college graduates prayed less, while in recent birth cohorts, they pray more or show no difference.

I will include just a few graphs to illustrate the general trends. Figure 13 shows the gap in evangelical Protestant identification. The negative bars indicate that those with a college degree are less likely to identify with an evangelical denomination. This gap was largest for those born in the

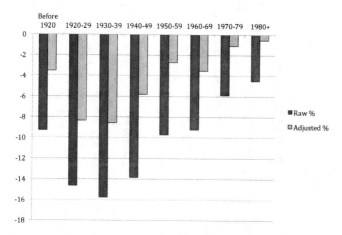

*Figure 13. The percentage point gap in evangelical Protestant affili-
ation between college graduates and everyone else by birth decade,
age 25+*
Source: GSS 1973–2012

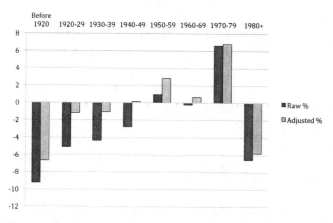

*Figure 14. The percentage point gap in belief in an afterlife between
college graduates and everyone else by birth decade, age 25+*
Source: GSS 1973–2012

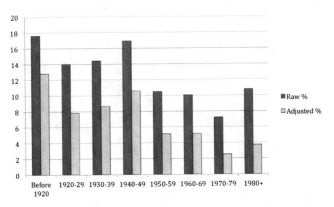

Figure 15. The percentage point gap in belief that the Bible is a "book of fables" between college graduates and everyone else by birth decade, age 25+
Source: GSS 1984–2012

1930s, but in recent decades, the gap is virtually non-existent once we control for the respondents' religious affiliation growing up. The next figure (Figure 14) shows the changing belief in an afterlife. There is a clear negative to positive trend in the data, indicating that college graduates from more recent birth cohorts are actually more likely to believe in an afterlife (there is a glaring exception for those born in the 1980s—but the sample size is much smaller here, so it is probably worth gathering a few more years of data before anything is concluded about a renewed secular influence from college among those born after 1980). Lastly, Figure 15 shows the changing gap in belief that the Bible is a book of fables. Although college graduates tend to be more likely to affirm this belief about the Bible, the adjusted gap (controlling for some religious measures growing up) is only about 2 to 4 percentage points in recent birth cohorts compared to about 13 percentage points for those born before the 1920s. In sum, most measures from the GSS seem to indicate that college had a greater secularizing influence for past generations, and, consistent with the other data we have been reviewing in this chapter, recent generations show a mixed religious influence from college.

Still another way to assess the historical impact is to compare two panel data sets (data that follow people over time) from different time periods. We have already examined some of the research that has used data from those born recently, but what if we look at a similar study from an earlier generation? The Youth Parent Socialization Panel Study began with a national sample of high school seniors in 1965 and followed up with them in 1973. Does college impact their faith trajectory from the first wave to the second? The answer appears to be yes. In models that control for some confounding factors, those who graduated from college in the late 1960s and early 1970s were nearly twice as likely to disaffiliate as those who did not graduate. They were also substantially more likely (about two and a half times) to believe the Bible was *not* divinely inspired. Interestingly enough, the typical positive influence of higher education on church attendance is absent in these data. College graduates were no more likely to attend church than those who never went to college. These findings provide further evidence that, yes, college most likely had a secularizing influence for past generations.

CONCLUSION

Summing up, in this chapter we reviewed social science data on the influence of college and found that, despite concerns about the secularizing influence of higher education, college tends to have a few positive impacts (in

the form of institutional belonging and practice) and a few
negative effects (in terms of certain super-empirical beliefs),
but primarily has no influence on religious faith. This can
even be said for those who are highly religious and those
who attend secular institutions. By most accounts there is
no mass defection from the faith in which college students
were raised. Also, by most accounts, religiously affiliated
colleges and universities—particularly evangelical ones—
tend to be doing a better job nurturing faith than public
institutions. Lastly, we examined the changing influence
of college on faith over time. Although we often lack the
historical data we need, we can use long-standing surveys
to provide good estimates of the changing impact of higher
education, with most items pointing to college being a
greater secularizing influence in the past than it is today.

3

Blinding Them with Science

I n this chapter we will examine another frequently voiced concern about young people: they are leaving the Church because of seeming conflicts between religion and science. Some in the Church believe that the youth are being corrupted by the secular agenda of elite scientists. These concerns are typically about the age of the earth and the origins of humans, and the critiques generally assume that Christians are unthinkingly accommodating to the anti-Christian assumptions inherent in mainstream science. Others in the Church are concerned that young people might be leaving for the opposite reason: they have been ill prepared in their Christian upbringing to deal with mainstream science. In this account young people cannot reconcile the position of their denomination or congregation to what they have learned and consequently leave the Church over the perceived conflict. Is either of these descriptions correct? Once again, we can turn to recent social science research to assess how well these accounts square with what we are finding out.

Science and Religion in Conflict

First, it would be good to know whether young people believe science and religion are incompatible at some level. A recent study that relies on the National Study of Youth and Religion finds that about two-thirds of 18 to 23 year olds believe that the teachings of science and religion are in conflict. Perhaps somewhat surprisingly, those who are

more religious on a number of measures are *less* likely to
believe there is conflict. This has been found to be true in
the general population as well. Another study that examined different religious groups found no differences in the
tendency to seek out scientific knowledge. Conservative
Protestants, for example, were as likely to be pro-science
as anyone else. Where they differed from other groups is in
their opposition to what they perceived as the moral agenda
of elite scientists in public debates. The science itself is not
framed as the problem.

Even if religious young people see less conflict between
religion and science than others, perhaps going to a secular
college or university still teaches emerging adults that such
a conflict exists (and that they should side with science).
After all, college professors, on the whole, are more secular
than the American population. Won't they indoctrinate the
young? Once again, we find no evidence that this is going
on. Using data from the Spirituality in Higher Education
project, a recent study finds that most incoming undergraduates do *not* report that they think science and religion
are in conflict. Not only this, but by their junior year, when
asked this survey question again, they are slightly *less* likely
to mark the conflict options than two years earlier. Even if
the overall trend is toward compatibility, perhaps majoring
in the natural sciences causes some to move to a conflict
position that favors science over religion. The results, once
again, clearly tell us this is not the case. Majoring in the
natural sciences had no relationship to a change in views
about the relationship between religion and science.

Let us take this one step further. Perhaps college, and
the natural sciences in particular, do not generate hostility
toward religion or the belief that science and religion are in
conflict. But maybe the natural sciences undermine religion

more subtly. Is it possible that students do not realize that
their beliefs and practices are being altered, but we can still
find evidence that they are? Once again, there is no evidence
this is happening. Using the same data, another study compares change over time in several measures of religiousness
and spirituality in college students. Put simply, the analysis
shows that majoring in the natural sciences appears to have
no negative impact on changes in multiple measures of spirituality and religiousness when compared to other majors.

HUMAN EVOLUTION

While it is reassuring to know that any perceived conflict
between science and religion is not associated with leaving
the faith or some of the other declines covered in the first
chapter, we all know where the conflict really lies: evolution.
Trying to square human evolution with the early chapters
of Genesis—or perhaps avoiding squaring evolution with
the early chapters of Genesis—is at the heart of the matter.
There is little doubt that this is a very important part of the
conflict thesis for the general public (for both atheists and
conservative Christians), but this book is about understanding the actual consequences of this perceived conflict.

There are two important components to this perception. On the one hand, we should expect to find that young
people who reject human evolution feel pressured to accept
it because of science education—which would be assumed
in either of the "faith crisis" models that the chapter began
with. On the other hand, we should anticipate that those
who change their views on human origins over time would
feel pressure to change their religious commitments as a result. Let's begin with the first scenario. Studies that rely on
a pre-test and post-test of students taking biology courses

in both high school and college find that most individuals
are resistant to changing their beliefs about human origins.
Some studies find a very small increase in acceptance of evolution, while others find no change. An even better way to
assess this is to rely on the national panel data we have been
using. The NSYR includes questions about evolution in both
Wave 2 (age 16 to 20) and Wave 3 (age 18 to 23); this allows
us to see who changes their views, what is associated with
this change, and what the consequences of changing views
are. To begin, those who reject evolution in the NSYR must
be pretty certain of their belief. To count as creationists, they
must affirm that "it is not possible" that God used evolution—and the question is posed to them exactly in this way.
Does going to college put pressure on young creationists
to change this view and instead accept evolution? According to the NSYR data, it does not. In fact, creationists who
attend a four-year (nonreligious) college or university are *less*
likely to change their belief than individuals who never go
to any college (although the differences are not statistically
significant). Sixty-two percent of creationists maintain their
rejection of evolution over time if they go to college, versus
56 percent of those who never go to college (Figure 16). This
pattern is not altered even when adding in numerous religious controls (as seen in the adjusted percent).

Still another way to assess this issue is to ask people
directly whether: (a) they learned about human evolution
in high school or college, and (b) whether this caused them
to change their belief. I have done just this as part of a national survey on human origins that I conducted for the Bi-
oLogos Foundation. What do we find? In a sample of more
than 3,000 US adults, fully 85 percent of creationists report
not changing their beliefs about human origins despite
learning about human evolution in high school. Ninety-one

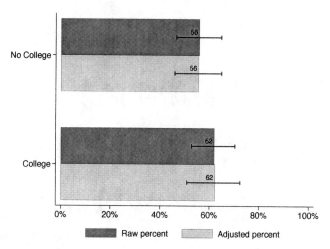

Figure 16. The percentage of creationists at age 16–20 who maintain
their creationist beliefs at age 18–23 by college attendance
Source: National Study of Youth and Religion 2002–3, 2005,
2007–8

percent of creationists who learned about evolution in college report not changing their beliefs.

This resistance to change because of science education
seems to indicate that most young creationists are *not*
being set up for a crisis of faith, despite rejecting mainstream science on the point of evolution. The second part
of the faith crises model supposes that those who *do* switch
their beliefs away from creationism will either strengthen
their faith (because they will relieve the tension between
their beliefs and mainstream science) or weaken their faith
(because they will acquiesce to the naturalistic assumptions
in mainstream science). For the most part, neither conjec-
ture is true; although in a few instances, there is evidence
that faith becomes less important when someone comes

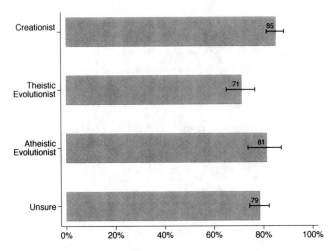

Figure 17. Percent reporting that they did not change their beliefs about human origins after learning about evolution in high school
Source: National Study of Religion and Human Origins, 2013

to accept the possibility of evolution. In these instances, church attendance drops more precipitously and self-rated importance of faith also declines. Doubts about one's faith also increase slightly more when a creationist comes to accept evolution. Other aspects, like beliefs in miracles, angels, and the frequency of prayer are not changed. But are these shifts really the result of a crises of faith brought about by the secular scientific establishment? We saw before how little secular science education in high school or college influences creationists, so what is going on here?

CONSTRUCTING BELIEFS

To better understand these data, we need to think more sociologically about the problem. It is often assumed that

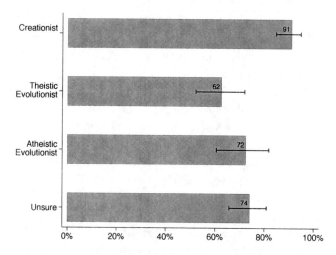

Figure 18. Percent reporting that they did not change their beliefs about human origins after learning about evolution in college
Source: National Study of Religion and Human Origins, 2013

people embrace certain beliefs through the rational weighing of information—sometimes referred to as the Bayesian model of belief construction. People weigh the information they have received and determine the probability that statement x is true; if they receive new information, the probability of x is adjusted accordingly. However, as a model for understanding how human beings actually come to accept or reject knowledge about the world, this is demonstrably wrong. Studies in the sociology of knowledge emphasize how our particular social location—the bundle of social identities and group memberships that give us our unique place in the broader society—shapes even our most "common sense" interpretations of the world around us. What seems natural and normal to us cannot be assumed to be so for others. We all belong to communities of belief that influence how we see our world. Consequently, we will work hard to maintain certain interpretations of the world against threats—because our very identity and social relationships are at stake.

These findings should help us understand what is going on with beliefs about human evolution in particular. Recent studies in cognitive science have emphasized the importance of non-rational mental mechanisms in the acceptance or rejection of beliefs about human pre-history. One recent study emphasized the importance of affective "gut" reactions in student understanding of evolution. Another showed that a sizable portion of the college student population values affective epistemic goals (i.e., believing what "feels" right) over goals of accuracy. Psychologists label this mixture of affect and reasoning "motivated reasoning." The reason why human evolution conjures up particular emotions has to do with its broader function of providing social identity and group belonging (and the reason this occurs is largely because of certain trajectories in American religious history). This means that where you land on this issue says significantly more about who you are and where you belong in the socio-religious landscape than what you believe about most other scientific issues. For most students, then, it matters little what their professor teaches. No amount of education is likely to persuade most pupils one way or another. What their friends, parents, and pastor think is going to be far more important, because their social world is inextricably tied up with these significant others.

When people change their beliefs about human origins, it usually will be found alongside other social changes: Friendship networks, relationships with family members, and participation in certain religious communities are altered as well. It is much more plausible that these social changes are actually the driving force in changing beliefs about the relationship between science and religion. In other words, framing the significant change about beliefs regarding human origins as primarily an intellectual puzzle which individuals deal with in isolation (which is true of both the models that began this chapter) is *not* the best way to understand the problem. While that model may be true for a select few people who are seriously engaged in the intellectual debates about science and religion, for the vast majority of young people, this is simply not how they arrive at their beliefs.

CONCLUSION

To sum up, although many young people believe that religion and science ultimately conflict with one another, there is no evidence that they feel pressure to change their beliefs because of science. The supposed crisis of faith brought about by mainstream science and certain readings of the early chapters of Genesis simply does not exist for most young people. While this doesn't discredit the instances where a crisis of faith is clearly brought about by this tension, it simply means this is not a widespread challenge for most young people. People come to accept or reject evolution not as a result of pouring over the details and evidence, but as a symbolic gesture to indicate to others where they belong in the socio-political landscape. This requires understanding that religious beliefs, and beliefs about other contentious public issues, are intertwined with identity and social relationships. Formal science education, for most young people, is unlikely to change this.

Conclusion

The Long and Winding Road to Adulthood

A s we have seen, pronouncing religious doomsday scenarios for today's youth should be avoided. The data, at first glance, appear to support a sizable exodus of emerging adults from the Church, but upon closer inspection we see that the matter is complex. Discontinuity with past generations of young Christians has almost certainly been overemphasized in popular accounts, although we do see real generational decline among Catholics. It seems to me that we should ask ourselves why the doomsday scenarios seem to carry such appeal. Perhaps it is simply carelessness or lack of social science training, although I think this is unlikely (and uncharitable). Let me suggest three other potential factors that may be leading us to frequently bias our interpretations.

First, our own social experience strongly colors how we frame the problem and interpret the data, yet our personal experience can frequently be an unreliable guide. We are often unaware of how deeply our particular social location—our race, social class, religious identity, friendship networks, etc.—influences our perceptions of the world. Information is filtered through a particular lens, which often leads to systematic biases. As a brief example, many Americans believe that violent crime rates have been rising in recent years; in fact, violent crime has substantially declined since the early 1990s. Homicide rates are half what they were in 1991 and are not markedly different from the rates of the 1950s. All violent crime has been declining, yet public perception of crime—largely filtered through mass media and politicians—is systematically in error. I would argue that church members assessing the current situation of young people might have similar distortions. Their own experiences—the circulating stories of individual faith struggle, the organizations that members are involved with, the new spiritual movements people hear about—almost certainly cause them to overestimate the prevalence of novel change. And while there may be some truth to these accounts, the reports are probably too quick to emphasize versions that are actually atypical and at the margins. Careful analysis of good social science data can help to correct these types of biases.

Second, generating crises in the Church can be an efficient and effective way to mobilize the faithful to action. Sociologists who study how social movements become successful have turned their attention in recent decades to how elites "frame" their message. Elites must work on generating an interpretational framework that identifies a specific problem, then identifies the source(s) of the problem, and finally provides a potential solution in the form of collective action. Further, the entire interpretational framework must align with existing grievances in recruits, otherwise collective action will fail. The temptation, then, will be for leaders in the Church to frame concerns about the next generation of Christians in such a way as to result in action by the rank and file, even if these interpretations are not entirely accurate.

Last, there is a fairly large gap between the ideal concept of Christian faithfulness and the "lived religion" of ordinary believers. For example, if we accept a basic measure of faithfulness to be (1) participating regularly in worship, (2) claiming that faith is important in daily living, (3) reading the scriptures at least somewhat regularly, and (4) praying at least fairly frequently, then probably only about 5 to 10 percent of adolescents and emerging adults in the United States meet this definition. Adding measures of orthodox belief would result in this number no doubt shrinking further. If we begin by analyzing this small remnant, it is easy to construct a secularization account that imagines some sort of golden age of orthodoxy that we have fallen from. The truth is that we have little evidence of such an age. Although the temptation is to believe that our present situation must be the result of religious decline, the historical and sociological case is far from watertight.

The bottom line is this: our judgment is pushed and pulled by a number of social forces of which we may not be consciously aware. Good social science can provide a check against some of our more egregious errors.

SOCIAL SCRIPTS

Nevertheless, emerging adulthood is a less religious period of life than either childhood or later adulthood. Why is this so? If you ask young people why they have stopped practicing their faith, you will find that most have not given much thought to the issue. In fact, asking such questions can be rather frustrating for researchers. The adolescents and emerging adults that gave in-person interviews as part of the National Study of Youth and Religion were, on the whole, very inarticulate about their faith. Most simply did not know why their behavior or beliefs had changed (if they had). To help us better comprehend the "why" question, we need to understand that most of the time, everyone—emerging adults included—follows tacit social scripts. We know this because much of social life is patterned and predictable. Most people engage in a fairly narrow range of

behaviors, because our social scripts tell us how to behave
in certain situations, what others should expect from us,
and what we have the right to anticipate from others. These
are largely predefined for us. We may like to believe that
our own trajectory in life is self-made, but this is simply not
the case.

Two important characteristics of social scripts help us
understand the faith practices of emerging adults. The first
is that social scripts come embedded within institutions.
We learn these scripts from our family, schools, churches,
and the mass media. Not only do we pick up these scripts
from social institutions, the social institutions legitimate
the scripts. In other words, they give them power and make
them compelling and real to us. We are largely assigned
scripts from these institutions and most individuals adopt
the culturally dominant scripts by default. We are not free
to "shop" for scripts.

The second important point is that the scripts themselves come packaged in sets of cultural practices. We do
not learn scripts the same way we memorize the periodic
table of elements. We both learn and enact them below
the surface of conscious thought most of the time. The
accumulation of regular experiences (i.e., practices) in our
family, schools, and places of work implicitly tell us a story
about who we are and where we are going. It is analogous
to the way most of us learn the rules of grammar. We
don't know why a sentence is wrong; we just know that it
is. There are unwritten rules we have picked up through
repeated exposure to correct grammar. The fact that we
cannot articulate these rules does not mean that they do
not exist and hold sway over how we write.

There is, for most emerging adults, a "faith script."
The culturally dominant faith script (manufactured by the

dominant social institutions in our society) implicitly tells young people that faith is primarily about being a good and happy person. One of the main findings from the National Study of Youth and Religion was that the primary function of faith is to provide basic moral guidance and help lead one to general life satisfaction. One might suppose that moral guidance would be something that most young people would desire as they navigate the various obstacles to becoming a full-fledged adult, but as it turns out, this basic morality is something many young people believe they already have a good handle on. The golden rule sums it up nicely for most. This means that religion is something useful for children, but it is of minimal use, at best, in steering through the twists and turns of emerging adulthood. Many emerging adults believe they will return to the Church (and many do), but only after these other transitions are behind them.

There are a number of other elements in this dominant script, but this description gets at the gist of it. Because it is the default mode for many young people, it is rarely reflected upon. This means that when you ask emerging adults why they have stopped going to church, the most common answers are non-answers. They will tell you they just don't know. They will say they have just drifted away. Most are not angry with the Church—certainly, you will hear some complain about hypocrisy or intolerance, but that is part of the script as well. Open hostility is rare. At the same time, not everyone follows the dominant script. There are minority versions of it as well. But such variations have the burden of counter-narrating this dominant script.

THE RESPONSE OF THE CHURCH

So the question at hand is this: How does the Church
provide a compelling counter-narrative to the dominant
script? I do not have programmatic suggestions for youth
ministries or anything of this sort. But I do think those who
are invested with leading the youth of the Church need to
reflect more deeply on what the dominant narrative currently is and how it is carried along in cultural practices.
James K.A. Smith calls these cultural practices secular
liturgies. They mimic the Christian liturgy, but instead of
practices that continually redirect our desire to its proper
source, these secular liturgies contain practices that twist
our desire toward the idols of our age. The pressing question, then, is how can we appropriate Christian liturgies in
such a way as to directly challenge the culturally dominant
faith script?

This needs to go beyond simply making Christianity
"relevant" for young people. After all, that approach too
often baptizes the very practices that need to be countered.
Popular music, television, and film are frequently viewed
as neutral mediums that simply need their secular content emptied out (e.g., bad language, violence, and explicit
sexual content) and replaced with "Christian" content.
Instead of singing about desiring a girl, the Christian pop
song sings about desiring God. What this approach fails
to recognize is that the very *form* taken by popular culture
often contains tacit pictures of the good life and human
flourishing. The structure and conventions of a Hollywood
action movie, or a romantic comedy, teach us to see the
world around us through a particular lens.

This suggests that an important strategy might be to
directly address some of the deeper cultural reasons for

emerging adult declines in faith as part of programs aimed at youth. Can young people learn to discern the dominant cultural messages they are receiving? Can they "read" the tacit cultural liturgies out there? This doesn't equate to a blanket condemnation of popular culture—surely that is as wrong-headed as blindly mimicking popular culture—rather it is an attempt to make young people *aware* of these unwritten social scripts. What, for example, does mass consumerism tell us about the good life? Does it matter that one of the ways we primarily conceive of ourselves is as consumers of goods? Is that at odds with Christian conceptions of the self and human flourishing? What about political involvement? Does it matter that many Christians relate to public life through political narratives that thrive on demonizing certain segments of society in order to win public influence? What sort of political culture do those patterns reinforce? What alternatives might there be for Christians in public life? Probing these sorts of questions could open up an awareness of the hidden side of cultural practices—practices that many young people believe to be morally neutral but that may, in fact, be shaping them in ways counter to how they should be formed for Christian worship.

Some of the best research indicates that a portion of this must happen at home. One of the most powerful predictors of whether young people continue to participate in church during emerging adulthood is whether they were raised in a home that made a habit of talking about and practicing their faith routinely. Although many parents might feel they have little influence over their teen's life, whether faith has been a central and routine part of a household really does generate a huge difference when young people eventually leave home. There is not another social institution that can

replicate the sheer amount of time and the overall emo-
tional investment of the family. Those who run church programs need to be partnering with parents to make sure that
faith is a regular part of home life. A weekly youth program
simply cannot compete with the influence of the home.

Still, even if young people learn to "read" the dominant
cultural liturgies of our time, and are raised in households
that teach the language of faith, this will do little to form
their faith if it is not accompanied by regular practices that
counter the dominant cultural liturgies. Keeping young
people involved in the heart of worship is the most important way to cast doubt about the dominant narratives
they receive from outside the faith. The church is a place of
Christian worship, and worship is something to which *all* of
God's people are called. Church is not about learning how
to be a moral person (though that is what the dominant
narrative they hear tells them); it is a place where immoral
individuals go in order to receive the grace of God. It is a
place where a people collectively profess how they have
fallen short and are collectively pardoned though the cross.
Worship places the gospel of grace at the center of life. It is
a necessary source of continual sustenance for the Christian, not an optional add-on to faith. After young people
learn to reflect on consumer culture or political practices,
Christian worship is where they will find the *strength* to
counter the raw will-to-power of the political realm and
the misplaced loves of the market. By continually retelling
these stories and embodying these practices, Christian
worship is what models an alternative to the dominant
faith script.

We all need to ask this question: how can we involve
emerging adults in our own congregations? The reason
they leave cannot be laid at the feet of higher education

or perceived conflicts with science. Nor can we say that Millennials are an alien species that are entirely different than generations that have come before. No, the patterns we see tell us that the sources of the decline in emerging adulthood faith have been built up over some time. Some of the social forces may be stronger than they were a generation or two ago, but they are not new. These pressures tell most young people that their faith is a personal preference that has little to do with institutions. They tell them that faith is primarily about moral guidance in life. And, because of all of this, emerging adults come to believe that church is good for young children and families, but not for them during this season of life. The only way to combat this is through recognizing, and countering, the ways that these beliefs were formed. Thankfully, there is a deep well of Christian teachings and practices that work to do just this. As we ponder how to deal with the contemporary challenges of emerging adults, perhaps it is time to turn away from the latest marketing technique and toward this ancient wisdom.

Notes

Series Editor's Foreword

vii **Midway along the journey of my life:** the opening verse of
The Inferno by Dante Alighieri, trans. Mark Musa (Blooming-
ton and Indianapolis: Indiana University Press, 1995), 19.

viii **We are always on the road:** from Calvin's 34th sermon on
Deuteronomy (5:12–14), preached on June 20, 1555 (*Ioannis
Calvini Opera quae supersunt Omnia*, ed. Johann-Wilhelm
Baum et al. [Brunsvigae: C.A. Schwetschke et Filium, 1883],
26.291), as quoted by Herman Selderhuis (*John Calvin: A
Pilgrim's Life* [Downers Grove, IL: InterVarsity, 2009], 34).

viii **a gift of divine kindness:** from the last chapter of Calvin's
French version of the *Institutes of the Christian Religion*. Titled
"Of the Christian Life," the entire chapter is a guide to wise
and faithful living in this world. (John Calvin, *Institutes of
the Christian Religion, 1541 French Edition*, trans. Elsie Anne
McKee [Grand Rapids: Eerdmans, 2009], 704.)

Introduction

3 **The pews of Protestant:** Emerging adulthood is the term
coined by the psychologist Jeffrey Arnett to mark the liminal
period after adolescence but before full-fledged adulthood.
This will vary from person to person, but we can think of
this period as roughly age 18 to 29. Jeffrey Arnett, *Emerging
Adulthood: The Winding Road from the Late Teens Through the
Twenties* (New York: Oxford University Press, 2006).

3 **Titles abound:** A sampling of some of these titles includes
David Kinnaman, *You Lost Me: Why Young People are Leaving
the Church...and Rethinking Faith* (Grand Rapids, MI: Baker

Books, 2011); Josh McDowell and David H. Bellis, *The Last Christian Generation* (Holiday, FL: Green Key Books, 2006); Drew Dyck, *Generation Ex-Christian: Why Young Adults are Leaving the Faith...And How to Bring Them Back*, (Chicago: Moody Publishers, 2010); Ed Stetzer, Richie Stanley, and Jason Hayes, *Lost and Found: The Younger Unchurched and the Churches that Reach Them* (Nashville, TN: B&H Publishing Group, 2009); Thom S. Rainer and Sam S. Rainer III, *Essential Church: Reclaiming a Generation of Dropouts* (Nashville, TN: B&H Publishing Group, 2008); Ken Ham, Britt Beemer, and Todd Hillard, *Already Gone: Why Your Kids Will Quit Church and What You Can Do To Stop It* (Green Forest, AZ: Master Books, 2009); Julia Duin, *Quitting Church: Why the Faithful are Fleeing and What to Do about It* (Grand Rapids, MI: Baker Books, 2009).

5   **"Millenials":** William Strauss and Neil Howe, *Generations: The History of America's Future, 1584 to 2069* (New York: Morrow, 1991).

5   **Generation Y:** Peter Sheahan, *Generation Y: Thriving and Surviving with Generation Y at Work* (Richmond, Australia: Hardie Grant, 2005).

5   **Generation Next:** Judy Woodruff, *Generation Next: Speak Up. Be Heard*, DVD (New York: Films Media Group, 2007).

5   **Echo Boomers:** Mark L. Alch, "The Echo-Boom Generation: A Growing Force in American Society," *Futurist* 34, no. 5 (2000): 42-51.

7   **While there are some:** Age, period, and cohort are linearly related to one another, making it impossible to fully separate out these effects using standard statistical procedures. See Norval Glenn, *Cohort Analysis, 2nd ed.* (Thousand Oaks, CA: Sage, 2005).

9   **Our personal knowledge:** Michael Polanyi, *Personal Knowledge: Towards a Post-critical Philosophy* (Chicago: University of Chicago Press, 1962).

10   **If there is a single complaint:** To be clear, I am primarily

critiquing the literature aimed at Christian audiences. There
is excellent work on this topic by academics, but much of this
work goes unread outside of academic circles.

CHAPTER 1

15   **By the time:** These statistics can be found on page 116 of
Christian Smith and Patricia Snell, *Souls in Transition: The
Religious and Spiritual Lives of Emerging Adults* (New York:
Oxford University Press, 2009)

17   **Also around 1990:** Actually, the latest figure from 2012 is 34
percent. The graphing method uses a smoothing technique
that averages together percentages from year to year in order
to better estimate general trends and give less weight to
potential outliers. Thirty percent is a conservative estimate.

19   **While the regular:** One might wonder why I did not split up
evangelical and mainline Protestant attendance into separate graphs (or at least show separate trend lines). I think
this would needlessly complicate their interpretation. In
recent years, very few 18-29 year olds are regularly attending
a mainline Protestant congregation (typically somewhere
between 1 and 2 percent). While these congregations may
not be appealing to young people, their "market share" has
also seen steady decline relative to other Protestant groups.
Separating out changing market share—the "availability" of
mainline Protestant congregations—from individual theolog-
ical orientation is not possible in these graphs. The primary
takeaway from this graph should be that 12 to 13 percent of
non-Catholic emerging adults are regular attenders, and this
has been the case since at least the 1970s.

21   **Some have argued:** This argument is most clearly articulated in N.J. Demerath III, "Cultural Victory and Organizational Defeat in the Paradoxical Decline of Liberal
Protestantism," *Journal for the Scientific Study of Religion* 34
(1995) :458-69.

21   **At an organizational-level:** Michael Hout, Andrew Greeley,

and Melissa J. Wilde, "The Demographic Imperative in Religious Change in the United States," *American Journal of Sociology* 107 (2001):k, 468–500.

21 **Nearly half of marriages:** These statistics come from Naomi Schaefer Riley, *'Til Faith Do Us Part: How Interfaith Marriage is Transforming America* (New York: Oxford University Press, 2013). Similar statistics can be found on pp. 148ff of Robert D. Putnam and David E. Campbell, *American Grace: How Religion Divides and Unites Us* (New York: Simon & Schuster, 2010).

21 **Political scientists:** See p.526 and p.531 in Putnam and Campbell, *American Grace.*

22 **Young people:** The most detailed account of this can be found in Robert D. Putnam, *Bowling Alone: The Collapse and Revival of American Community* (New York: Simon & Schuster, 2000).

23 **Even if we look:** These figures are both calculated from the National Study of Youth and Religion Data (Wave I and Wave III).

23 **this is hardly:** For example, see the Lifeway Research data reported in Thom S. Rainer and Sam S. Rainer III, *Essential Church: Reclaiming a Generation of Dropouts* (Nashville, TN: B&H Publishing Group, 2008), 2–3. Also see Drew Dyck, *Generation Ex-Christian: Why Young Adults are Leaving the Faith... And How to Bring Them Back* (Chicago: Moody Publishers, 2010), 17.

23 **It is well documented:** Ross M Stolzenberg, Mary Blair-Loy, and Linda J. Waite, "Religious Participation in Early Adulthood - Age and Family-Life Cycle Effects on Church Membership," *American Sociological Review* 60 (1995): 84–103.

24 **These self-reports:** C. Kirk Hadaway, Penny Long Marler, and Mark Chaves, "What the Polls Don't Show: A Closer Look at U.S. Church Attendance," *American Sociological Review* 58 (1993): 741–52.

24 **Longitudinal data:** For a more detailed analysis of the

Catholic and Protestant differences in church attendance, please consult pp.51–59 of Christian Smith, Kyle Longest, Jonathan Hill, and Kari Christoffersen, *Young Catholic America: Emerging Adults In, Out of, and Gone from the Church* (New York: Oxford University Press, 2014).

25 **Even the concept:** Kent Baxter, *The Modern Age: Turn-of-the-Century American Culture and the Invention of Adolescence* (Tuscaloosa, AL: University of Alabama Press, 2011).

26 **Public practice:** See Rodney Stark, "Secularization, R.I.P," *Sociology of Religion* 60 (1999): 255–60.

26 **cohabiting before marriage:** According to the 2002 National Survey of Family Growth, around half of 15 to 44 year old males and females report having ever lived with an unmarried partner of the opposite sex. See http://www.cdc .gov/nchs/nsfg/abc_list_c.htm#currentcohab. If we restrict this to 19 to 44 year olds, 58 percent of women report having cohabited. See Richard Fry and D'Vera Kohn, "Living Together: The Economics of Cohabitation," (Washington, D.C.: Pew Research Center, June 27, 2011).

26 **never marry:** Eric Klinenberg, *Going Solo: The Extraordinary Rise and Surprising Appeal of Living Alone* (New York: Penguin, 2012).

CHAPTER 2

29 **The general finding:** For a summary of these studies see Kenneth A. Feldman and Theodore M. Newcomb, *The Impact of College on Students, Volume 1* (San Francisco: Jossey-Bass, 1969), 23–28.

30 **They are no more likely:** See Philip Schwadel, "The Effects of Education on Americans' Religious Practices, Beliefs, and Affiliations," *Review of Religious Research* 53 (2011): 161–82.

32 **For the most part:** For further reading (and more detail about the data and statistical modeling that goes into these assessments) please consult the following journal articles:

Jeremy E. Uecker, Mark D. Regnerus, and Margaret L. Vaaler, "Losing My Religion: The Social Sources of Religious Decline in Early Adulthood," *Social Forces* 85 (2007): 1676; Jonathan P. Hill, "Higher Education as Moral Community: Institutional Effects on Religious Participation During College," *Journal for the Scientific Study of Religion* 48 (2009): 515–34; Damon Mayrl and Jeremy E. Uecker, "Higher Education and Religious Liberalization Among Young Adults," *Social Forces* 90 (2011): 181–208; Jonathan P. Hill, "Faith and Understanding: Specifying the Impact of Higher Education on Religious Belief," *Journal for the Scientific Study of Religion* 50 (2011): 533–51.

32   **I examined:** With so many statistical tests, it is possible to generate one or two "false positives" (known as Type I errors). So, while the general patterns I describe are, I believe, essentially correct, it is important not to place too much emphasis on any one finding.

32   **university faculty:** Neil Gross and Solon Simmons, "How religious are America's college and university professors?" SSRC Web Forum on the Religious Engagements of American Undergraduates, http://religion.ssrc.org/reforum/Gross _Simmons.pdf (accessed December 19, 2014); Elaine Howard Ecklund, *Science vs. Religion: What Scientists Really Think* (New York: Oxford University Press, 2010).

33   **Sociologist Tim Clydesdale:** Timothy T. Clydesdale, *The First Year Out: Understanding American Teens after High School* (Chicago: University of Chicago Press, 2007).

33   **Similarly, Donna Freitas:** Donna Freitas, *Sex and the Soul: Juggling Sexuality, Spirituality, Romance, and Religion on America's College Campuses* (New York: Oxford University Press, 2008)

34   **The bottom bar:** Along with church attendance during adolescence, I control for religious tradition, frequency of prayer, frequency of Bible reading, importance of faith in daily life, parents' income, parents' education, closeness to parents, whether they attended a religious high school, gender, race/ ethnicity, age, and census region. These all are measured when

the respondent was an adolescent. I also control for whether they are living at home or not when they are age 18 to 23.

35   **The disenchantment:** W. Bradford Wilcox, Andrew J. Cherlin, Jeremy E. Uecker, and Matthew Messel, "No Money, No Honey, No Church: The De-institutionalization of Religious Life Among the White Working Class," *Research on the Sociology of Work* 23 (2012): 227-50.

35   **Marriage and family life:** For an account of this among whites, see Charles Murray, *Coming Apart: The State of White America 1960-2010* (New York: Crown Forum, 2012).

38   **Those determined:** For an overview of campus parachurch organizations, see John Schmaulzbauer, "Campus Ministry: A Statistical Portrait", SSRC Web Forum on the Religious Engagements of American Undergraduates, http://religion.ssrc .org/reforum/Schmalzbauer.pdf (accessed December 19, 2014).

38   **Christian Smith:** Christian Smith, *American Evangelicalism: Embattled and Thriving* (Chicago: University of Chicago Press, 1998).

39   **I think the answer:** For example, Charles Stokes and Mark Regnerus have conducted a review of the research on colleges that belong to the Council for Christian Colleges and Universities (a network of evangelical, liberal arts colleges) and reached a similar conclusion. The difficulty is that much of the existing research really does not properly isolate the impact of CCCU institutions in their methodology. Higher quality studies will be necessary to really establish the impact of certain types of institutions or certain types of students. Charles E. Stokes and Mark D. Regnerus, "The CCCU and the Moral and Spiritual Development of their Students: A Review of Research," http://www.cccu.org/filefolder/2010Forum _Wed-_Delivering_on_Our_Promises_CCCU_Moral __Spiritual_Development_-_Full_Report_1.doc (accessed December 19,2014).

39   **The Spirituality in Higher Education survey:** http:// spirituality.ucla.edu/

41   **Not only this:** Alexander W. Astin, "The Changing American
      College Student: Thirty Year Trends, 1966–1996," *Review of
      Higher Education* 21 (1997): 115–36.

41   **Two sociological:** Dean R. Hoge, Jann L. Hoge, and Janet
      Wittenberg, "The Return of the Fifties: Trends in College
      Students' Values between 1952 and 1984," *Sociological Forum*
      2 (1987): 500–519; David O. Moberg and Dean R. Hoge, "Cath-
      olic College Students' Religious and Moral Attitudes, 1961 to
      1982: Effects of the Sixties and Seventies," *Review of Religious
      Research* 28 (1986): 104–117.

45   **In models:** Jonathan P. Hill, "Religious Pathways during the
      Transition to Adulthood: A Life Course Approach" (Ph.D.
      diss., University of Notre Dame, 2008).

CHAPTER 3

49   **These concerns:** See, for example, Ken Ham and Greg Hall,
      Already Compromised (Greenforest, AZ: Masterbooks, 2011).

49   **In this account:** For an example of such an account, see
      http://biologos.org/blog/evolution-and-faith-my-journey
      -thus-far.

49   **A recent study:** Kyle C. Longest and Christian Smith, "Con-
      flicting or Compatible: Beliefs About Religion and Science
      Among Emerging Adults in the United States," *Sociological
      Forum* 26 (2011): 846–69.

50   **This has been found:** Joseph O. Baker, "Perceptions of
      Science and American Secularism," *Sociological Perspectives* 55
      (2012): 167–88.

50   **After all, college professors:** Gross and Simmons, "How
      Religious Are America's Professors"; Ecklund, *Science vs.
      Religion*.

50   **the Spirituality in Higher Education project:** http://
      spirituality.ucla.edu/

50   **a recent study:** The differences between the NSYR and the
      Spirituality in Higher Education data are probably due to

different phrasing of the question. The NSYR asked respondents their level of agreement that the teachings of religion *ultimately* conflict with each other and another question asked for their agreement that the teachings of religion and science are *entirely* compatible. The Spirituality in Higher Education provided four closed-ended responses about the relationship between science and religion. Respondents had two "conflict" options (one which they could side with religion and the other which they could side with science) and two non-conflict options (one in which they are considered independent of each other, and one in which they collaborate and support one another).

Christopher P. Scheitle, "U.S. College Students' Perception of Religion and Science: Conflict, Collaboration, or Independence? A Research Note," *Journal for the Scientific Study of Religion* 50 (2011): 175–86.

51   **Using the same data:** Christopher P. Scheitle, "Religious and Spiritual Change in College: Assessing the Effect of a Science Education," *Sociology of Education* 84 (2011): 122–36.

52   **Some studies find:** All of the following studies use this method to assess acceptance of evolution: Ella L. Ingram and Craig E. Nelson, "Relationship between Achievement and Students' Acceptance of Evolution or Creation in an Upper-Level Evolution Course," *Journal of Research in Science Teaching* 43, no. 1 (2006): 7–24.; Justin W. Rice, Joanne K. Olson, and James T. Colbert, "University Evolution Education: The Effect of Evolution Instruction on Biology Majors' Content Knowledge, Attitude toward Evolution, and Theistic Position," *Evolution: Education and Outreach* 4, no. 1 (2011): 137–44; Anton E. Lawson and William A. Worsnop, "Learning about Evolution and Rejecting a Belief in Special Creation: Effects of Reflective Reasoning Skill, Prior Knowledge, Prior Belief, and Religious Commitment," *Journal of Research in Science Teaching* 29, no.2 (1992): 143–66; Beth A. Bishop and Charles W. Anderson, "Student Conceptions of Natural Selection and Its Role in Evolution," *Journal of Research in Science*

Teaching 27, no. 5 (1990): 415–27; Anusuya Chinsamy and Eva Plaganyi, "Accepting Evolution," *Evolution* 62, no.1 (2007): 248–54.

52   **Ninety-one percent:** See pp.24–29 of the report on National Study of Religion and Human Origins, http://biologos.org /uploads/projects/nsrho-report.pdf

54   **Other aspects:** Due to space constraints, these figures are not included in the book. They are available upon request from the author.

54   **It is often assumed:** Nick Chater and Mike Oaksford, *The Probabilistic Mind: Prospects for Bayesian Cognitive Science* (New York: Oxford University Press, 2008).

56   **Consequently, we will work:** For a similar social psychological account, see Michael W. Magee and Curtis D. Hardin, "In Defense of Religion: Shared Reality Moderates the Unconscious Threat of Evolution," *Social Cognition* 28 (2010): 379–400.

56   **One recent study:** Minsu Ha, David L. Haury, and Ross H. Nehm, "Feeling of Certainty: Uncovering a Missing Link between Knowledge and Acceptance of Evolution," *Journal of Research in Science Teaching* 49 (2011): 95–121.

56   **Another showed:** T.D. Griffin, "Individual Differences in Epistemic Goals and the Acceptance of Evolution," in *Proceedings of the Twenty-ninth Annual Conference of the Cognitive Science Society*, eds. D.S. McNamara & J.G. Trafton (Mahwah, NJ: Erlbaum, 2007), 1765.

56   **Psychologists label:** Kunda Ziva, "The Case for Motivated Reasoning," *Psychological Bulletin* 108 (1990): 480–98.

56   **The reason:** For an excellent account of how creationism became a successful social movement in the United States, see Michael Lienesch, *In the Beginning: Fundamentalism, The Scopes Trial, and the Making of the Antievolution Movement* (Chapel Hill, NC: University of North Carolina Press, 2007).

56   **This means:** See Jon D. Miller, Eugenie C. Scott, and Shinji Okamoto, "Public Acceptance of Evolution," *Science* 313 (11

August 2006): 765–66. Miller et al. demonstrate that religious and social conservatism have stronger predictive influence on what people believe about human evolution in the United States than in nine European countries in a cross-national study. They believe this is precisely because of the highly political nature of the issue in the United States.

Conclusion

61 **Homicide rates . . . 1991:** http://www.fbi.gov/about-us/cjis /ucr/crime-in-the-u.s/2010/crime-in-the-u.s.-2010/tables /10tbl01.xls

61 **the 1950s:** http://bjs.ojp.usdoj.gov/content/homicide/tables /totalstab.cfm

62 **Sociologists:** David A. Snow, E. Burke Rochford, Jr., Steven K. Worden, and Robert D. Benford, "Frame Alignment Processes, Micromobilization, and Movement Participation," *American Sociological Review* 51 (1986): 464–81; Robert D. Benford, "Framing Processes and Social Movements: An Overview and Assessment," *Annual Review of Sociology* 26 (2000:, 611–39.

62 **if we accept a basic measure:** Smith and Denton *Soul Searching*, 220; Smith and Snell, *Souls in Transition*, 259.

63 **The truth is:** See Rodney Stark, "Secularization, R.I.P".

63 **The adolescents:** Smith and Denton, *Soul Searching*, 118–71; Smith and Snell, *Souls in Transition*, 143–65.

63 **To help us:** For a use of the concept of social scripts to understand emerging adult sexual behavior, see Mark Regnerus and Jeremy Uecker, *Premarital Sex in America: How Young Americans Meet, Mate, and Think about Marrying* (New York: Oxford University Press, 2011), 4.

64 **These are largely:** A prime example of this can be found in Annette Lareau, *Unequal Childhoods: Class, Race, and Family Life*, 2nd ed. (Berkeley: University of California Press, 2011). Lareau powerfully demonstrates how social class and family

life constrain the future trajectories of youth in predictable ways.

65   **One of the main findings:** Smith and Denton, *Soul Searching*, 124–27. Smith and Snell, *Souls in Transition*, 148–50.

65   **There are a number:** Chapter 4 of Smith and Denton, *Soul Searching*, and chapter 5 of Smith and Snell, *Souls in Transition* summarize a number of dominant themes that emerge through extended interviews with teenagers and emerging adults.

66   **James K.A. Smith:** James K.A. Smith, *Desiring the Kingdom: Worship, Worldview, and Cultural Formation* (Grand Rapids, MI: Baker Academic, 2009).

67   **Is that at odds:** William T. Cavanaugh, *Being Consumed: Economics and Christian Desire* (Grand Rapids, MI: Eerdmans, 2008).

67   **Does it matter:** James Davison Hunter, *To Change the World: The Irony, Tragedy, and Possibility of Christianity in the Late Modern World* (New York: Oxford University Press, 2010), 106–7.